Darlene's Workshop

Darlene's Workshop Presents

Dollhouse Accessory Workbook

Volume 1

Polymer Clay Jewelry and Trinket Boxes

By Darlene A. Gregory

DAG Publications, LLC.
Rutland, Vermont

Disclaimer: The instructions and methods given in the book have been tested, and are presented in good faith. However, no warranty is given, and results are not guaranteed. DAG Publications Inc., disclaims any liability for injury resulting from the use of recommended tools and materials.

Copyright © 2018 by Darlene A. Gregory and DAG Publications LLC. All rights reserved. This book may not be reproduced in part or in whole without written permission from the publisher.

Printed in the United States of America

All photographs are by Darlene A. Gregory.

Darlene's Workshop

Darlene's Workshop

For Dad and Grandpa
Whose workshops inspired me
to have one of my own.

Contents

- Introduction 3
- Legal..Front
- Materials & Tools List..6
- Tips before you Start..4
- Basic Box Bottoms..11
- Wooden Trinket Boxes..11
- Adding Box Feet...19
- Painting the Outside of the Wooden Trinket Boxes...................25
- Attaching Box Hinge...21
- Painting the Inside of the Trinket Boxes...................................26
- Adding Mirrors...28
- Painting the Hinge..27
- Glass top Trinket boxes...31
- Making Patterned Box Sides...31
- Round Trinket Boxes..39
- Painting Tips..25
- Making Multiple Boxes...44
- Suppliers..47
- About the Author...48

Introduction

The use of Trinket and Jewelry boxes dates back many centuries.

The original Trinket boxes were were made in a multitude of sizes and shapes. They were constructed using everything from wood to porcelain to silver and even gold. Jewelry and Trinket boxes became popular around the world during the Victorian years 1873 – 1901. In the early 1900's the boxes took on a decidedly Art Nouveau look. From the fancy French Limoges porcelain boxes to the basic hand carved wooden boxes, from Kings to paupers, almost every household held a trinket box of some kind.

The smallest Trinket boxes were made to hold thimbles and embroidery scissors. The larger Trinket boxes were used to hold jewelry. The earliest Trinket and Jewelry Boxes were most often crafted by skilled artists and were considered almost as valuable as the jewelry they were designed to hold.

All these centuries later Trinket and Jewelry Boxes continue to be very popular and most certainly should be part of any well stocked dollhouse. Using the directions included in this book and your imagination you will be able to make any size trinket box you desire, in any dollhouse scale, from the popular 1/12 and 1/24 scales and beyond.

I hope you enjoy creating your own tiny boxes and letting your imagination run wild!

Chapter 1

Tips

Safety

Materials

Tools

and settings

TIPS and Safety Before you begin:

Remember to:

- Keep your hands and workspace clean of dust.
- Keep your polymer clay rolling machine clean.
- Knead your clay until it is soft and pliable before beginning work
- Ceramic tiles; I use several 5"x 5" ceramic tiles, originally intended for a bathroom wall, to work and bake my polymer clay items on. I like the smaller size but larger tiles work fine as well. Individual ceramic tiles can usually be purchased at your local big box hardware stores. You will want a tile(s) that has no texture and a gloss finish. Your clay will pick up any textures that are in the tile, so make sure there aren't any.

Tip: you can also use the bottom of a cookie sheet to bake your items. Purchase a cookie sheet that you will dedicate to use only for crafting.

Tip: many clay crafters place parchment paper under their clay creations when baking the items. It reduces shiny spots on the bottom of the clay. I did not use it for creating these trinket boxes.

Safety: Polymer clay is graded as non-toxic; however, as with all craft materials it is wise to use some simple precautions.

- Do not use polymer clay tools for preparing people food.
- Supervise children when they are using polymer clay.
- Do not allow polymer clay to burn. If you accidentally burn the clay, turn off the oven, open the windows and leave the area until the smell is gone.
- Using a separate oven thermometer is greatly recommended. Most oven temperatures are off by several degrees. When baking polymer clays, a few degrees under or over can make the difference between a fully cured piece or an over baked-burned mess.
- Do not leave un-baked polymer clay on wood surfaces or furniture. It will damage the finish.

Materials & Tools List

- White Polymer Clay
- Liquid Polymer Clay
- Clay rolling machine or rolling tools
- Cutting Tools; Tissue Blade aka Cane Cutter and a Straight Razor blade
- Clay Cutters; or items found around your home
- Needle tools, both round ended and pointed; toothpicks will work as well.
- Tweezers
- Bias Tape
- Oven for baking the polymer clay
- Beads and jewelry findings
- Water Based Clear Gloss Polyurethane or polymer clay glaze
- Baby Powder
- Ceramic Tile Work Surface; or a flat cookie sheet
- Acrylic Paints & paint brushes
- Mirror Effect Self Adhesive Contact Paper
- Fine Sand paper
- White Craft Glue that dries clear, Aileen's Tacky Glue © is recommended

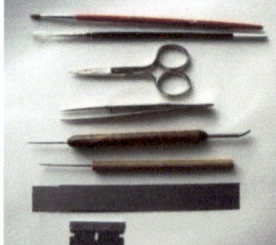
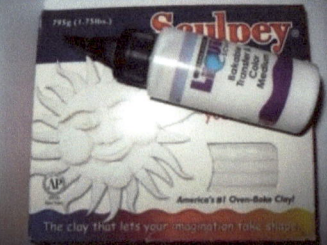

Collect some Findings, beads and Jewelry, to pattern your Trinket Box Tops

- You will need to find some items to use to press patterns into the clay for your trinket box tops and sides. You can use old jewelry, new jewelry, beads or filigree findings from any hobby store. Just about anything that has a pattern that is in scale to the size trinket box you want to make.

- I used a combination of new filigree, beads and metal antique jewelry findings to make the boxes in this book. You can also use plastic items but be aware that if you don't remove all traces of the clay from the plastic piece the plastic may react to the uncured clay. This usually means the uncured clay will eventually melt the original plastic piece.

Tip: If some of the clay sticks to your item, I find that gently brushing the item with an old toothbrush is helpful in removing any leftover clay from your findings.

General Clay Rolling Machine Settings:

- Box Tops and Box Bottoms; Set the clay rolling machine width dial to 4.

- Box Sides: Set the clay rolling machine width dial to 3.

Tip: You can also use a hand roller to roll out your clay. I find that the clay rolling machine will give you the best uniformity and thinnest clay for making these tiny trinket boxes.

- I used white polymer clay to make these boxes. I prefer to paint my boxes and I find that using the white clay allows me to layer the paint for a better depth of color. All of the boxes in this book were made using white Sculpey ©

Tip: There are stronger polymer clays available than the one used in this book. If you are making Trinket boxes for re-sale, or just want to create a stronger box, I suggest that you look into using a clay that cures to a harder finish like Premo ©. Adjust the baking temperatures to the directions on the package of the clay that you are using.

Darlene's Workshop

Chapter 2
Basic Box Instructions

The following wooden trinket box instructions include the instructions for the jewelry and trinket "Basic Box".

You will use these "Basic Box" instructions to create all of the other boxes detailed in this book.

I recommend that you start here and learn the basic details of how to build your jewelry and trinket boxes.

If you would like to begin with a different style of box you will be referred back to this chapter for several of the "Basic Box" in depth step instructions so you can complete your jewelry or trinket box.

Wooden Trinket Boxes & Basic Box Bottoms

- Condition your Clay: Take a walnut sized piece of clay from the box of clay and condition it by kneading the clay until its soft and pliable

- Box top and Bottom: Using the clay rolling machine, set the dial to #4. Roll out a sheet of the conditioned clay. The sheet can be as large or as small as your working surface.

    - (For very tiny boxes use thickness dial setting # 3 for both the tops and the sides of the boxes.)

- Lay the sheet of rolled clay onto your ceramic baking tile. (You can also use the bottom of a flat cookie sheet.)

- Slice off the rough edges of the clay to make it easier to work with.

- Sprinkle some baby powder over the top of the clay sheet and gently spread it over the surface with your finger being careful not to press and mark the clay with your fingers.

- Place your jewelry finding on the powdered clay and press it into the clay, creating a pattern.

- **Top of Box:** Center your clay cutter over the box top pattern and press down cutting into the clay.

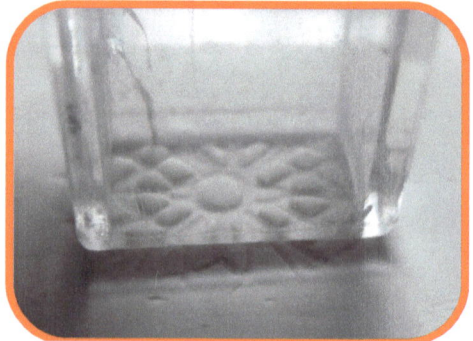

- **Bottom of Box;** Using the same clay cutter, cut a box bottom from a piece of un-patterned flat clay.

- **Free Hand Box Cutting:** You can also cut the box top and bottom free hand, using a razor blade or tissue blade. Be sure to cut the box bottom so it is the same size as the box top. Cutting free hand and using the instructions in this book, you can make any sized Trinket box that you desire in any size scale.

- **Prebake;** Remove the excess clay from around the box tops and bottoms. Leave them on the tile and Pre-bake the tops and bottoms at 275 degrees for 9 minutes. These can be pre-baked along with the side panels.

Tip: **Clay cutters** can be purchased in any craft store or you can use items found around your home. If you purchase your clay cutters be sure to buy a quality brand that has a good sharp square edge. I've found that many of the square clay cutters on the market today are not truly square, having rounded edges at the corners instead of sharply square edges.

- o Here are the "around the house" clay cutters that I used for some of my boxes. The square plastic clay cutter, in the photo on the left, originally held pencil lead and the one next to it on the right, was a tool cover found in my sewing machine kit box.

Around the House Cutters

Hand Cut

Tip: See page 44 for instructions on how to make multiple trinket and jewelry boxes at the same time.

Basic Box Sides and Keyholes:

- Using the clay rolling machine roll out a sheet of clay with the width dial set on #3.

- Lay the sheet of pressed clay onto your ceramic baking tile. It's okay if your clay sticks to the tile.

- Cut off the rough edges of clay.

- Powder the top of the Clay.

- Using a needle or ball ended tool press your keyholes into the clay. Make the holes approximately 3/4 to 1 inch apart, depending on the size of your boxes.

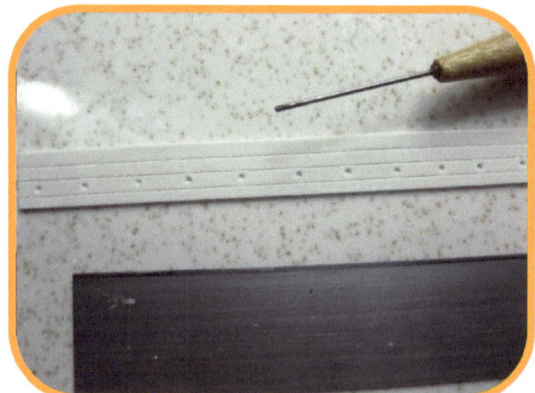

- Using the long flat Tissue Blade press down and cut straight lines into the clay. Cut all the way through the clay but don't lift or separate the strips. Carefully pat down any strips that have pulled up from the tile.

- Do not remove the clay strips from the tile until after pre-baking. These strips will be used for the sides of your boxes.

- Pre-bake the sides, tops and bottoms at 275 degrees for 9 minutes. Pre-baking the box pieces will make them easier to cut and assemble without warping the clay.

Tips:

- Make the lines as far apart as you would like the height of your box sides to be. Try different heights for different looks.

- If you forget to press the keyhole into the clay before pre-baking you can carefully carve it into the front box panel using an x-acto knife, although it may take a couple of tries and a couple of broken pieces. Do this before you put your box together.

- See the chapter on "Making Multiple Boxes" for directions on using a clay cutter instead of cutting the boxes free hand.

Approximate Box Dimensions: I hand cut the Trinket box used in these basic box instructions. Here are the final dimensions of the box. I'm not suggesting that you try to match these exact measurements. I'm just giving you an idea of the size of this box.

- Lid and box bottom; 3/4" long by 3/8" wide. (1.8 cm long by 1 cm wide)
- Box front sides; 3/16" High by 5/8" long. (1.5 cm long by .5 cm high)
- Box sides; 3/16" high by 2/8" long. (8 mm long by .5 cm high)

Attach the sides of the boxes.

- Carefully separate and pull away one of the pre-baked side pieces from the strips of clay.

- Using a straight razor cut the 4 box side panels from the pre-baked side strips.

- The length of your panels will be determined by the size of your box bottom. The front and back panels of the box should be cut slightly shorter than the box bottom length and width. (see photos)

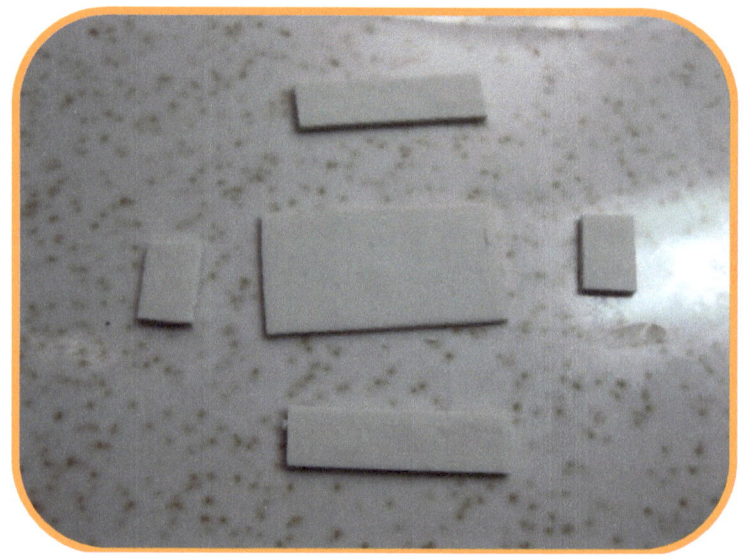

- Cut the front Panel from the strip with the keyholes. Cut the panel so that the keyhole is centered on the front of the panel.

- The two box sides need to be small enough to allow room for the back and front box panels, while still leaving room for the extra space on the front and back of the box. (see photo below)

Attach Back Box Side: Spread the liquid clay along the bottom edge of the back panel. Using tweezers, attach the back panel to the pre-baked box bottom. Be sure to leave a tiny lip along the back and sides of the box, see photo.

Attach Sides of Box: Next attach the right and left sides of the box by spreading liquid clay along the bottom of the side panel, as well as along the end of the side panel that will attach to the back of the box. Remember to leave a lip on the outside of each side panel. (See photo below on right)

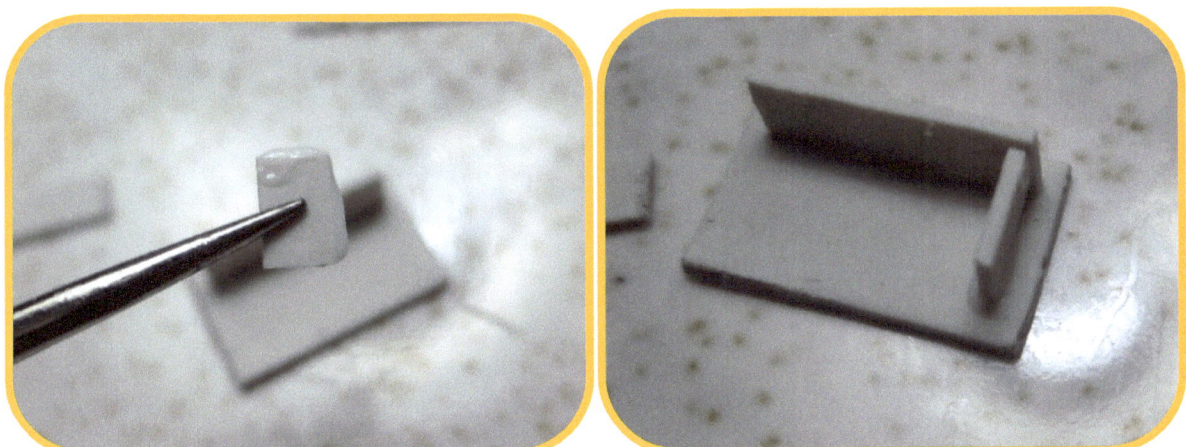

Attach front Panel: Attach the front box panel using liquid clay on the bottom of the panel and on the ends of the two side panels.

Tip: To make it easier for you to see the placement of the liquid clay in the photograph, I really gummed on the liquid clay in these photos. You will want to use less liquid clay. The more liquid clay that you use the more you will have to clean up before baking.

The liquid clay stays liquid until baked so you have time to move the panels around to make sure they are squared and in the correct position.

- If you put on too much liquid clay use a long needle tool or a straight pin to remove any extra liquid clay from the outside and inside of the box. Any liquid clay left on the box will bake solid onto the piece.

Final Bake: Fully bake your completed box. Don't place the box top on the box for this final bake. Doing so will risk the top sticking to the liquid clay on the box bottom and you won't be able to open it.

Bake at 275 degrees for approximately 15 minutes. Watch your pieces carefully during the final minutes of baking to be sure they don't over-bake or begin to turn brown. I highly recommend that you use an extra oven thermometer to be sure your oven is baking at the correct temperature.

Adding Box Feet

Flush or Offset:
- There are two ways to add feet to your boxes. One is to add them flush to the edges of the box and the other is to set them just outside the bottom edge of the box. Each way gives your box a different look.

Flush Feet vs. Side Feet:

- Here are the basic directions for adding box feet using the the flush edge.

- Using a fully baked strip of clay, cut 4 squares of the same size, using a sharp razor blade or clay tissue blade. Carefully sand any ragged edges using a very fine sand paper.

Attaching Baked Feet:
Using a white craft glue, attach the baked squares to the under side of the fully baked boxes, flush with the edges. Wipe off any excess glue. Using a needle tool or straight pin for this is helpful. Let dry.

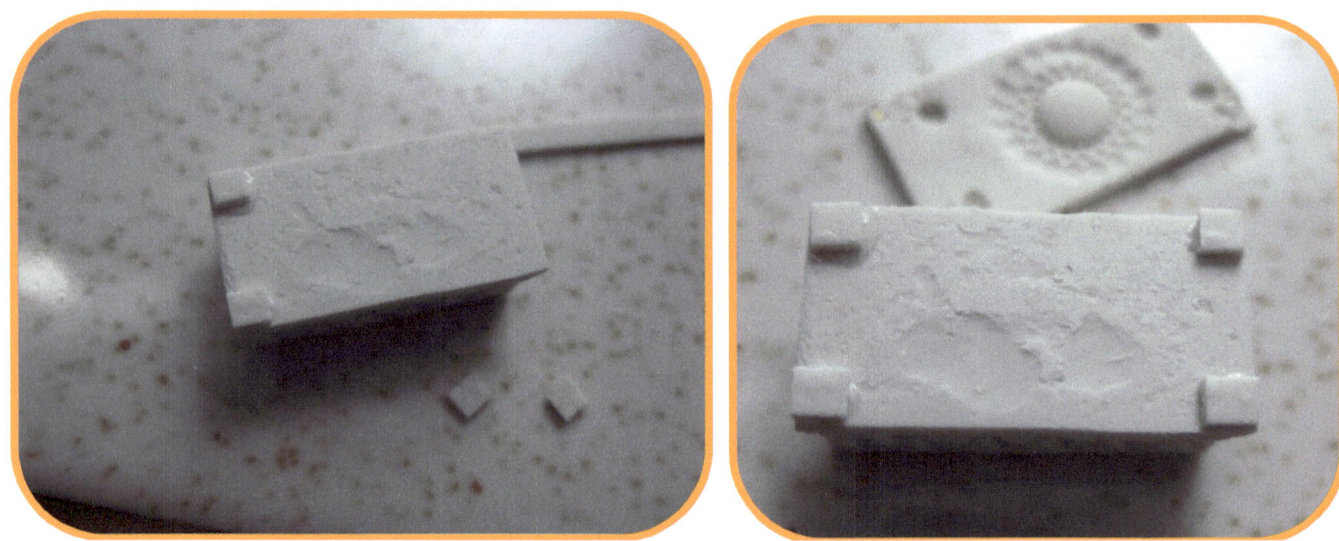

Tip: **Paint before or after adding the hinge?** You can paint your trinket box before adding the hinge, as I have done here, or you can wait until after the hinge is added.

Generally if you are not going to paint the hinge fabric inside the box you will want to paint the box before adding the hinge. See **"Painting Your Trinket Box"**, for painting instructions and tips.

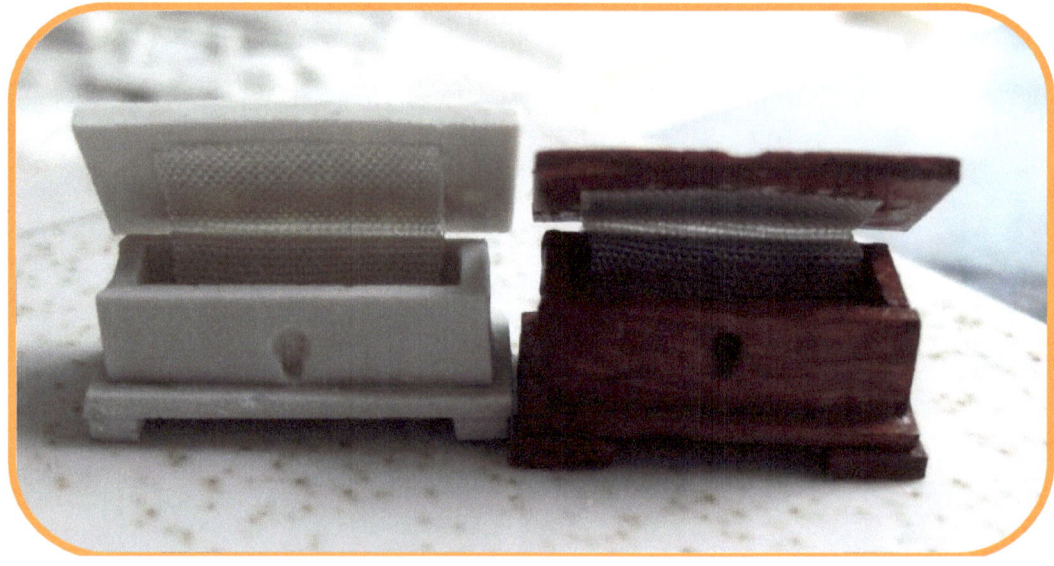

Attaching the Box Hinge

Bias Tape or Fabric Hinge

To make the box hinge, you will need bias tape, available in any fabric store. Bias tape is not really a tape. It's a fine piece of fabric used to make clothing. A very fine piece of fabric will work as well.

Tip: A polyester cotton blend bias tape will work, however, if you can find a silk bias tape it will be easier to fold and works better as a hinge on the smaller boxes. The stiffer the bias tape or fabric, the harder it will be to get the box lid to close. Ribbon tends to be too stiff and won't work properly with these tiny boxes.

- Using a small paintbrush, brush a coat of thick white craft glue on the bottom of the inside of the box and up along the back inside of the box and across the back top edge. I use Aleene's Tacky Glue ©

- Cut a strip of bias tape, two inches long. Match the width of the bias tape to the width of the inside of the box.

- Using needle tools or a toothpick, press the strip of bias tape onto the glue along the bottom of the box and then up along the back of the inside wall.

- Fold the ribbon back over the glue that is along the back top ridge of the box. Hold for several seconds until the glue catches the bias tape and it is well attached to the box.

- Remove any excess glue that may have oozed out.

- Allow the folded and glued bias tape to dry.

- When the glue on the back edge of the box is dry, carefully fold the bias tape forward, across the box. Using your finger, flatten the folded bias tape along the top edge of the box creating another crease.

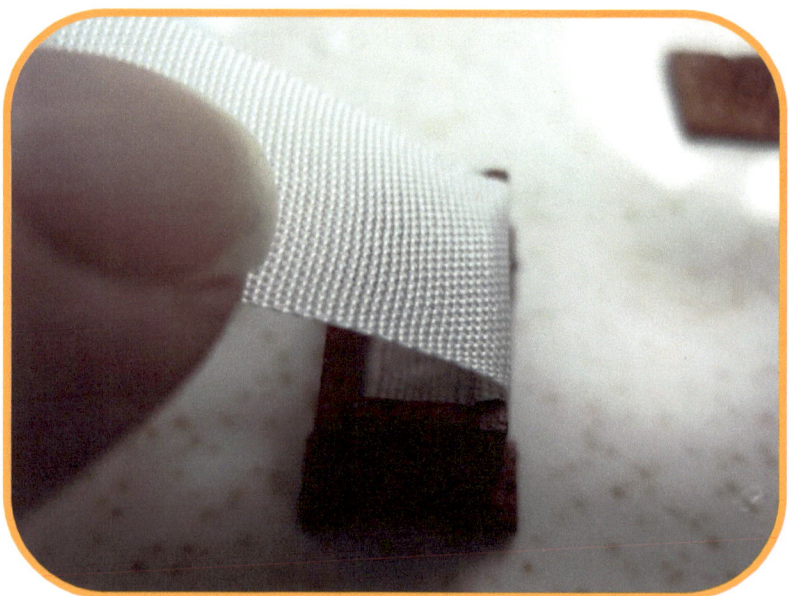

- Spread glue on the top of the folded and creased bias tape.

- Attach the box top by placing it upon the glued portion of bias tape

- Close the box and move the box top around on the glued tape until it is centered over the box bottom.

- Remove any excess glue that may have oozed out from underneath the bias tape.

- Open the box top a bit and allow the glue to dry.

- Once the glue is dry, use a sharp pair of scissors to cut the excess bias tape off of the box top. Cut the bias tape a bit back from the top edge of the box so that the box will close properly when finished.

Tip: See the "Glass Top Box" chapter page 35 to see photos and directions for adding a short hinge that uses less fabric.

Painting Your Trinket Box

Tips:
- Your boxes can be painted with any type of acrylic paints. For the best results, be sure to use a high quality acrylic paint with good pigments.

- When painting over your box designs remember that several lighter coats of paint are better than one thick coat that will hide the pattern you pressed into the box.

- Painting your box with a darker paint color and then dry brushing a lighter color over the top of the darker paint will highlight the pattern on the box. You can also use a watered down dark paint and wicking method to lowlight the design crevasses of a lighter paint color. This technique is similar to the Silver Trinket Box Paint instructions but with using a more watered down paint.

Wooden Box Paint:

- To paint my "wooden" trinket boxes I used FolkArt © brand Enamel Acrylic Paint #4135 Burnt Sienna.

- Paint the box side panels from left to right using a fairly stiff bristle brush. Using a stiff brush allows the paintbrush bristle strokes to show, giving the trinket box the look of wood grain.

- I do not add a polyurethane coat to my "wooden" boxes. Though adding light a coat of flat polyurethane will help to protect the paint.

The Bias Tape Hinge; Inside the Box

There are various ways that you can cover the bias tape hinge fabric inside the box.

- Paint the bias tape to match the color of your box.

- If you are going to add a mirror to the box top you can paint only the bias tape on the lid of the box and paint the bias tape inside bottom of the box the color of your choice.

- If you find a pretty fabric to use for your hinge you can skip painting the bias tape inside of the box altogether.

TIP: Many of the antique and vintage metal trinket boxes had silk or velvet fabric on the inside of the box. Although it is possible to find some very fine grained fabrics to use inside your boxes, I found that these tiny boxes were mostly too small to use real fabric on the inside.

Painting the inside of the box the color of velvet will give the look of fabric without stuffing the box full of an out of scale fabric.

Paint the Hinge:

- **Hidden hinge:** Paint the back edge of the box, where the bias tape shows, the same color as your box.

- **Metal look hinge**: You can also paint the hinge a gold or silver color to represent metal hinges. You can paint one long metal hinge or two short metal hinges.
To be honest these boxes are so tiny that, without a magnifying glass, most people won't even be able to see the gold hinges.

Adding Mirrors

Adding mirrors to your trinket boxes will also add another dimension of reality to the look of these tiny boxes.

Materials needed:
- ✓ Mirrored Contact Paper
- ✓ Small Pair of Scissors
- ✓ Glue

Cutting and Attaching the Mirror:

- Full Mirror: If you are adding a full mirror, cut the mirror so it is the same height and width as the inside of the box bottom. This will allow the box to close properly.

- Diamond Mirror: If you are adding a diamond shaped mirror, cut the mirror so that the diamond mirror is the same height, top to bottom, as the inside of the box. This will allow the box to close properly.

- Remove the paper from the back of the contact mirror paper.

- Add a small dab of glue to the backside of the mirror. Attach and center the mirror on the inside lid of the trinket box. Don't press too hard! These boxes can be delicate.

Tip: For these tiny boxes you could use a small piece of flattened aluminum foil instead of the mirrored paper. The effect won't be as mirror like but from a distance they will still look great.

Congratulations! You have finished your first Trinket Box! Don't be discouraged if it didn't turn out perfectly the first time. The first box is the hardest. As you can see here, my first box was large, clunky and completely out of scale for a dollhouse. My second box was much better and became my inspiration for this book.

One last thing before we move on is to be sure to sign and date your work! The bottom of the box is the perfect place. Future generations of dollhouse owners will love to know who crafted this lovely piece of dollhouse history and when.

Now that you have mastered the basic construction of a trinket box you have the skills to move on to the more detailed boxes.

Chapter 3
Let's Get Fancy, But First:

The upcoming jewelry and Trinket boxes use the Basic Box Bottom instructions that are detailed in Chapter 2 page 11.

You will be referred back to Chapter 2 Basic Box Instructions for directions on how to complete the following boxes.

Glass top Trinket Box

How to make Patterned box Sides

- Roll a sheet of clay through the clay rolling machine at a dial thickness setting of #3.

- Place the #3 sheet of clay onto a baking tile.

- Dust clay with powder.

- Roll or press a design into the sheet of clay.

Tip: don't press too hard when rolling or you will push holes through this very thin clay.

- After pressing in your pattern, cut the strips for the box sides using a flat blade or razor blade. This is the same technique that is used in the Basic Box chapter on page 14. For a patterned box side be sure to cut the clay strips so that the pattern is centered along the strip of clay.

- Using your Tissue blade carefully cut the raw clay into long strips and pre-bake. You will use these strips to make the sides of your glass box.

- Pre-bake the patterned strips, 275 degrees for 9 minutes.

- After pre-baking, carefully remove the strips from the tile and separate them.

- Cut the strips to match the 4 side lengths of your box, front, back and 2 sides. Attach the sides to the box bottom using polymer liquid clay. See the basic box bottoms instructions on page 16 for step by step instruction details.

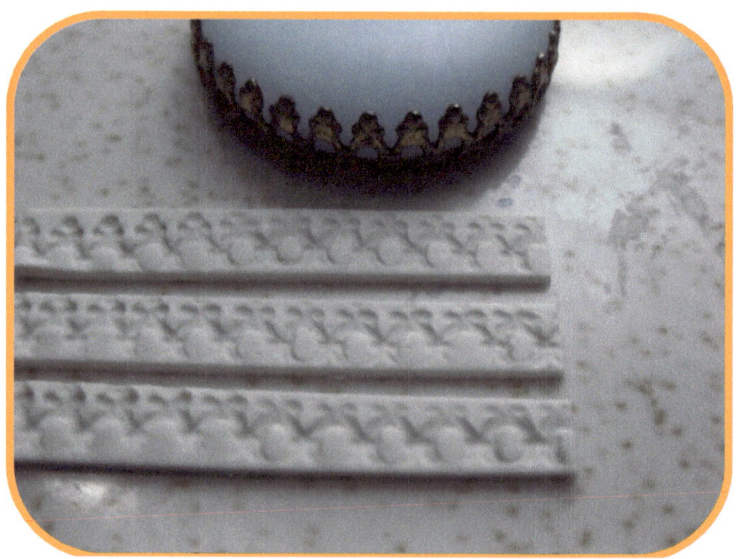

Making the "Glass" Top

- Using the clay roller, roll and cut some thin, plain clay strips, using a thickness dial setting of #3. Fully bake the strips, 275 degrees for 15 minutes. Watch them carefully to be sure they don't burn.

- From the baked strips, cut out 4 sides to match the size of your box bottom.

- Connect the sides together using white glue on the edges. It will look like a picture frame when finished.

- Wipe off any excess glue.

- Allow the glue to dry.

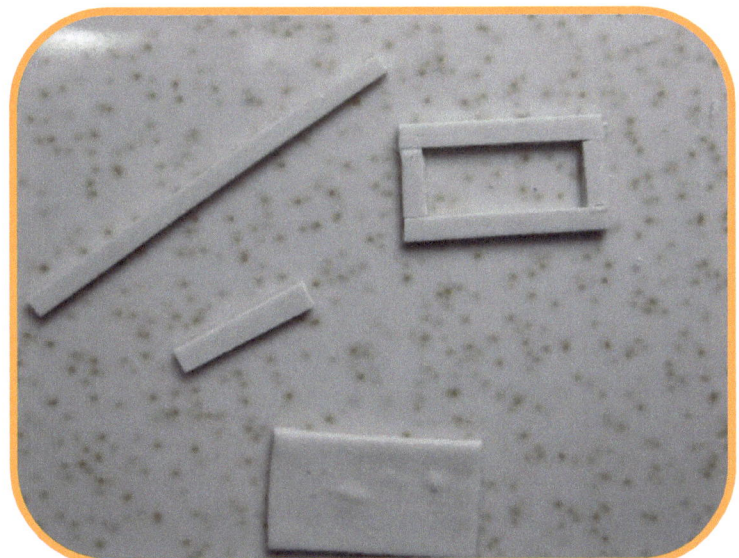

- Once the glue is dry paint the box lid frame and the bottom of the box. See the Copper Box Painting instructions on page 36.

- Allow paint to thoroughly dry.

- Cut a small piece of thin clear plastic to fit on the underside of the box top. This creates the look of a glass topped trinket box.

- You can purchase clear plastic sheets at most craft stores or use plastic found around the house. For this box, I actually used the clear plastic packaging from my bias tape.

- Using white craft glue that will dry clear, attach the plastic to the underside of the trinket box top.

    - Tip: Be careful to not get glue on any of the clear plastic that will be seen through the box top opening. Even though the white craft glue dries clear, in this tiny scale the glue will still be a noticeable blemish on the glass.

- Allow the glue to dry.

Attaching a Shortened Hinge

- Attach a shortened piece of bias tape to the back of the box. The instructions and folding are the same as if you were using a longer piece of binding tab. See, Basic Box Chapter 2; Attaching the Hinge, on page 21 for the detailed hinge instructions.

- Attach the "glass" lid to the box bottom using the shortened piece of the binding tape. The binding tape should be cut down short enough so that I won't be seen through the top of the glass box. See photos.

- Paint the binding tape to match color of your box.

Copper Box Painting:

- Paint your box with two light coats of copper metallic paint. I used Ceramcoat © Metallic Copper. Allow the paint to dry.

- Dry brush over the copper paint with a gold metallic paint. I used DecoArt © Extreme Sheen 24k Gold. Of course the paint isn't really 24k gold and any gold metallic paint will work.

- Lightly dry brush a second coat of paint over the gold dry-brushed paint using a very light coat of the copper metallic paint. Continue dry-brushing until you achieve the look you desire.

Tip: Dry brushing is a painting technique that is used in a lot of crafting. You simply coat your paintbrush with paint then, using a tissue or cloth, wipe off most of the paint from the brush. Leaving an almost dry brush. You then use the paintbrush to brush over your object leaving a small amount of paint that still allows the original paint to show through.

Brass Box Paint:

- Paint your box with two light coats of copper metallic paint. I used Ceramcoat © Metallic Copper. Allow the paint to dry.

- Dry brush over the copper paint with a gold metallic paint, until you achieve the brass color you want. I used DecoArt © Extreme Sheen 24k Gold.

- Add a light coat of Polymer gloss to the finished box.

Silver Trinket Box Paint:

- My silver boxes were painted with several thin coats of a highly pigmented acrylic silver paint. Allow the silver paint to dry between coats.

- Water down a tiny bit of black paint so that it is very liquid but still retains the black color.

- Using your paintbrush place a drop of the watered down paint onto the design pattern. The paint should quickly flow from the brush into the design crevasses of your pressed pattern.

- Use the corner of a tissue or piece of toilet paper to wick the extra watered paint away, leaving the black paint only in the crevasses of the design.

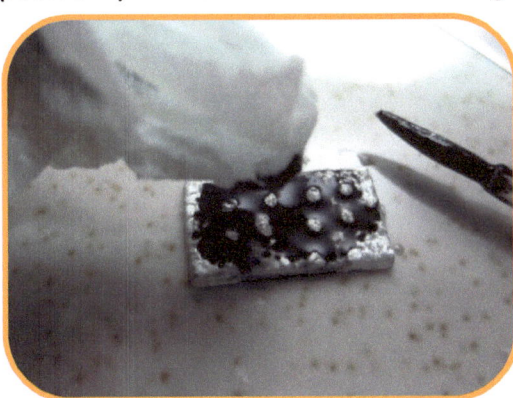

- When the black paint is completely dry cover the box with one or two coats of water based, clear gloss Polyurethane. When completely dry, add the hinge.

Black Laminate Box Paint:

- Paint your box with one or more coats of black acrylic paint. I also use black paint on the inside of the box and on the hinge when creating these boxes.
- Allow each coat of black paint to dry completely.
- Using a tiny paint brush you can add colors and detail to your box design.
- Allow the detail paint to dry completely.
- Paint the box with one to two coats of water based, clear gloss Polyurethane.

Tip: Detail colors can be added before or after adding the Polyurethane. When the detail paint is fully dry add another thin coat of the Polyurethane gloss over the part of the box that you painted with detail paint.

Chapter 4
Round Trinket Boxes

Make the Tops and Bottoms for the Round Trinket Boxes:

To create round trinket boxes, use a round cutter to cut out the top and bottom of the boxes. You can purchase round clay cutters, or find something around your house that will work just as well. I used both the purchased cutters and a small round glass jar, which formerly held some seed beads, to create these boxes.

- Using the clay rolling machine, roll out a sheet of clay with a dial thickness of #4. You will cut both your round box tops and box bottoms from this clay.

- Spread a fine layer of baby powder on the top of the flattened clay.

- Using your finding, press your pattern into the clay.

- Dip your round clay cutter into some baby powder. Tap off any extra powder, leaving a light film of powder on the cutter.

- Keeping the clay pattern centered under the cutter, press the cutter into the clay cutting out the circle for your box top.

- Remove the excess clay from around the clay cutter.

- Using the same clay cutter tool, cut a plain clay circle for the bottom of the box.

- Pre-bake the top and bottom of the round jewel box. 275 degrees for 9 minutes.

- After baking, use a sharp knife or razor blade to carefully remove any extra excess clay from around the edges of the box top and bottom.

Round Box Sides: For a round box, you must use <u>unbaked clay</u> for the sides of the trinket box.

- Set the clay roller machine dial at #4 and roll out a sheet of clay. Pressed designs in the round box sides require using this thicker sheet of clay, as you will be manipulating the raw clay to create your box sides.

- Press your design into the clay.

- Cut the clay strip to the size that you want for the sides of your box. Tall or short. It's up to you and your imagination.

- Carefully bend the clay strip around the base of the trinket box, along the inside of the circle edge. Leaving a lip all around the outside of the box, just as you would leave in the Basic Box Bottom directions.

Tip: Be sure to place the clay on the inside of the box bottom, creating a ledge/lip. Don't place the clay around the outside of the box. If you do your box top will not fit the box.

- Using your tissue blade carefully cut the excess clay off of the end.

- Once the strip of clay is cut to the correct length, spread a thin layer of liquid clay along the bottom of the strip.

- Using your needle tools, carefully place and arrange the sides around the box base.

- Attach the ends of the clay together using liquid clay.

- Do a final bake of both the top and bottom of the trinket box, 275 degrees for 15 minutes. Be careful not to over bake.

- Paint your baked trinket box before or after adding the hinge.

Adding a Smaller Hinge to a Round Box
- Add a smaller strip of binding tape to attach the top of the box. Cut the hinge and fold it the same as in the folding instructions in the Basic Box Bottom chapter on page 21.

- Paint the binding to match the interior of the box.

Chapter 5
Making Multiple Boxes at one time

Multiple Box Bottoms:

- Roll two sheets of #3 conditioned clay and place them on the tile.
- Powder the clay.
- Using your clay cutter, press cut multiple bottoms.
- Remove the excess clay that is around the pressed box bottoms.
- Carefully flatten any bottoms that have lifted from the tile.

Multiple Box Tops:

- Roll two sheets of #3 conditioned clay and place them on the tile.
- Powder the clay.
- Press multiple patterns into the clay.
- Center your clay cutter over the pattern and press cut the clay box tops.

- Before baking, remove the large pieces of excess clay from around the box tops.

- Don't try to remove any flattened clay edges that form just around the outsides of the cut out box tops and bottoms. You will trim that off after the pre-bake. See photo

- Carefully flatten any clay tops or bottoms that have lifted from the tile.

- Pre-bake your trinket box tops and bottoms, 275 degrees for 9 minutes.
- After baking, carefully use a razor blade or x-acto knife to remove any excess clay from around the box top and box bottom edges.

- Cut and prepare the sides and feet for your boxes using the Basic Box directions in Chapter 2.

- Refer to the Basic Box instructions in Chapter 2 to complete your trinket boxes.

Finish

I hope you have enjoyed learning how to create these wonderful dollhouse miniatures.
Using the techniques provided in this book and your imagination, you can make any size trinket or jewelry box in any scale that you can imagine.

You are only limited by your imagination.

You can fill your boxes with miniature jewelry, candy, bits and baubles or leave them empty and use them for decoration.

Be on the look out for other dollhouse miniature books from Darlene's Workshop.

Suppliers

- Self Adhesive mirror reflection paper; available at Amazon.com
- Round clay cutters; available at most hoppy and craft stores.
- Tissue /clay cutters; available at most hobby and craft stores.
- Clay rolling machine; also available at most hobby and craft stores.
- Aileens tacky glue; available at most hobby and craft stores.
- Sculpey; available a most hobby and craft stores

About the Author

Darlene Gregory has been creating her own miniatures, dolls and craft items since she was a young girl.

Her passion for teaching people how to make their own craft items began at age 12 when she was searching for a way to learn how to make her own plaster doll molds. At the time there was no internet in her area and living in a small town the local library had very little to offer for instruction.

She decided then and there that she would always make sure to share whatever she learned with the world so they could learn from her techniques and bring their own creations to life.

Ms. Gregory has always been drawn to clay, whether the clay was porcelain, ceramic or polymer. This first series of dollhouse accessory books will concentrate on instructions for making items using polymer clays.

Index

About the Author	48
Attaching Box Sides	16-17
Baking; Final Box Bake	18
Basic Box Bottoms	11
Before you Begin	5
Black Laminate Box Painting	38
Box Feet; Adding	19-20
Box Hinge; adding	21-24
Box Hinge; Painting	26-27
Box Sides	14
Box Sides; Attaching	16-17
Box Sides; Round boxes	41
Boxes; Round	39-43
Brass Box Painting	36
Tools	4
Clay Cutting	12-13
Clay Rolling Machine Settings	8
Contents	2
Copper Box Painting	36
Final Box Bake	18
Findings for Box Tops	7
Patterns; Beads and Findings	7
Finish	46
Free Hand Clay Cutting	12
Glass Top Trinket Box	31-35
Hinge; Shortened	35
Index	49
Inside the Box	26
Introduction	3
Keyholes	14-15
Machine Settings	8
Materials and Tools List	6
Mirrors, Adding	28
Multiple Boxes; making	44-45
Paint; Black Laminate Boxes	38
Paint; Silver Boxes	37
Painting the Hinge	27
Painting Your Wooden Trinket Box	25
Painting; Brass Boxes	36
Painting; Copper boxes	36
Patterned Box Sides	31-32
Pressing Patterns into Clay	12
Round Box Sides	41
Round Boxes	39-43
Safety	5
Shortened Hinge	35
Silver Trinket Boxes	37
Suppliers	47
Tools List	6
Top of Box	12
Wooden Box; Painting Box	25
Wooden Trinket Boxes	11

www.ingramcontent.com/pod-product-compliance
Lightning Source LLC
Chambersburg PA
CBHW041833170426
43191CB00045B/43